bagne
or
Criteria for Heaven

by rob mclennan

books:
Notes on drowning
bury me deep in the green wood
Manitoba highway map
The Richard Brautigan Ahhhhhhhhhh
bagne, or, Criteria for Heaven

chapbooks (selected):
some breaths
harvest
cranial devices (advice to myself (last poems
bagne
a song about Nelson Ball
the wiser
*had i written a poem about Montreal
        it would have looked / like this*
last leaves
dead city radio
we live at the end of the 20th century
Poems from the Blue Horizon

anthologies:
Poetry Nation
Open 24 Hours

editor:
Shadowy Technicians: New Ottawa Poets
Written in the Skin
FREE VERSE

bagne

or
Criteria for Heaven

rob mclennan

edited by
Judith Fitzgerald

Fredericton • Canada

bagne, or, Criteria for Heaven copyright © 2000 by rob mclennan.

Design and in-house editing by Joe Blades
Cover art © 2000 Tom Fowler/Big Bug Illustration, Ottawa

No part of this publication may be reproduced, stored in a retrieval system or transmitted, in any form or by any means, without the prior written permission of the publisher or, in the case of photocopying or other reprographic copying, a licence from the Canadian Copyright Licencing Agency (CAN©OPY), 1900-One Yonge St, Toronto ON M5E 1E5. Ph (416) 868-1620, 1-800-893-5777, admin@cancopy.com www.cancopy.com

Printed and bound in Canada

The Publisher gratefully acknowledges the support of the Canada Council for the Arts and New Brunswick's Arts Development Branch for its eligible title publishing program.

This book has been simultaneously published by our eBooks imprint (ISBN 1-896647-39-1) in a digital PDF binding with distribution by PublishingOnline.Com

Broken Jaw Press

Box 596 Stn A
Fredericton NB E3B 5A6
Canada

www.brokenjaw.com
tel / fax 506 454-5127
jblades@nbnet.nb.ca

Canadian Cataloguing in Publication Data
McLennan, Rob. 1970-

    Bange, or, Criteria for Heaven

    Poems.
    ISBN 1-896647-32-4

I. Fitzgerald, Judith. II. Title. III. Title: Criteria for heaven.

PS8575.L4586B34 2000   C811'.54   C00-950115
PR9199.3.M33413B34 2000

fr joanne & douglas
fr judith
fr gb

God is not invited to take part in future civilization.
 — *Le Devoir*, 20 nov 1948

much thanks to Judith Fitzgerald for the brilliant edit.

some of these poems have appeared in *The Journal of Canadian Literary Stuff*, *The Cafe Review*, *The Carleton Arts Review*, *The Danforth Review*, *Dig*, *Laughing Gland*, *Qwerty*, *Queen Street Quarterly*, *The Tulane Review*, various above/ground press **poem** broadsheets, the chapbook *bagne* (Calgary: House Press, 1999), on Gerry Gilbert's *Radio Free Rainforest* (Vancouver Co-op Radio) & CHUO's *artsnack*.

jwcurry: you can't start with the title, can you?

chris kubsch: i think so

jwcurry: well you can, yeah it's true. but i dont know, if you start with a title, in a case like this, it would tend to direct things, rather than leave things open

> — *the jwcurry experience*

rob mclennan

bagne

one	13
1. to lie down with and rest	14
2. the petals of aptly faded hope	15
3. the ghost of Freda Capshaw	16
4. I can raise the dead	17
5. unravelling another millennium of mystery	18
6. turning and turning in the wide silent sky	19
7. the slight halt that rests in your words	20
8. hidden in its sheath of air	21
9. salt of her primal sea	22
10. The Distances We Travel By Night	23
11. more in love with you than ever	24
12. the skeleton of a little girl turning	25
13. I only shoot to kill	26
14. that was love but I kept on travelling	27
15. here the rectangular sky opening up shh	28
16. there are no divided hearts	29
17. heard only the lament of crows	30
18. Perhaps the gods are returning	31
19. you paint snow falling	32
20. impossible love	33
21. but you were always ambitious	34
two	35
22. blowing a new day into a new season	37
23. sadness becomes me	39
24. the other eye the final hieroglyph	40
25. least of minstrels	41
26. in the wake of spring	42
27. like sunlight on the wings of birds	43
28. into remarkable clouds	44
29. winter when our minds fill up with snow	45
30. sharp as stainless steel	46
31. and how we slowly began to look like her	47
32. with dark coming on and the cold	48
33. giddy during the earthquake	49
34. how tired the ashes are. what weight in a rose?	50

bagne, or, Criteria for Heaven

35. japan in my own language	51
36. how little a dead person bleeds	52
37. Those indelible blue solitudes	53
38. peddling clouds like bicycles	54
39. the melancholy tango of the rain	55
40. The other side, the mountain gag	56
41. as if life could touch its metaphors	57
42. to follow the frightening shape of their desires	58
43. & revenge w/ the speed of light	59
44. Everything open gets filled, gets closed	60
45. There are no rules anymore	61
46. shards, fragments, deitrus	62
47. looking for what has been lost	63
48. they lie with me in a common grave	64
49. things do happen emma laraine's daughter smiling due november	65
50. the sound of our own steps over the high green meadows	66
51. We are deep in the centre, fixed and very slow	67
52. a place lighted only by your eyes	68
53. I do not think I am thinking	69
54. that these songs go unfinished	70
55. he says a name for water	71
56. did his magic for him, suddenly	72
57. waiting for a rescue hours overdue	73
58. Made by her passage through the open lanes	74
59. Be in danger. Look.	75
three	77
60. and it's like someone escaping that we run to mere breathing	79
61. you and the portrait that I see	80
62. like the waving handkerchiefs of kings	81
63. sorrow side	83
64. i'll get on the next ferry when it reaches me."	84
65. away into the dark lake forever	85
66. The moon is a tear caught by a tongue	86
67. weaving their invisible ways	87
68. for you just two steps short of the measure	88
69. In your painting, it's a soundless dark space	89
70. possibility in this place, in your body, here.	90
71. He's had it up to here.	91
72. to sew in her tongue	92
73. like a moon among all these things	93

four	95
74. you must make to survive.	96
75. where silent, unrefractive whiteness lies.	97
76. The name is the bullet.	98
77. secretly more for himself than his reader	99
78. is burning burning burning burning up.	100
79. and am nearing home	101
80. means what it does not, and more's the pity	102
81. the perfect ending to their perfectly ordinary evening.	103
82. and the sun keeps coming...	104
83. for a little linseed oil and a chamois	105
84. to the portal? Advance still backwards yet more?	106
85. In the distance there is the distance	107
86. in my lonely house, I'm drunk on passion again	108
87. in secret places I hide my fat and wait for rain for rain for rain	109
88. your shame, white veil, or the peace of God	110
89. I will know from the inside out	111
90. the silence — my stories are of no consequence	112
91. waiting and waiting to finish what she started.	113
92. the dream dreaming itself out of control	114
93. the small pieces of her go.	115
bagne: postcript	117
about the author	118
about the cover artist	119

one

I've been downhearted baby
ever since the day we met

— Primitive Radio Gods

bagne, or, Criteria for Heaven

1. to lie down with and rest

fr victor coleman

      sliding over
    the collapse of the east
in a sunshine village
canadas largest gravel quarry
      eroding
    every time we look
a growth
  & pipeline fawcett
tho brian only in one discussion
two
    marking the hands
that feed
    mutual give
almost impossible
to work out from under

a creation myth
of self & epic proportion

rob mclennan

2. the petals of aptly faded hope

fr lisa robertson

    dismissing virtue
as an altered fact,
the ghost of a particular time

fingering up & down your posture,
our combined weight shifting
      under cultur'd pop

 & into the next era,
    a domino effect, marias
   three white men
  or where the
     dollar stops
/a pile of necessity

a bag of new two-dollar coins
    stolen & untraceable
w/ the shift from paper & the serial trail

finding a way of leaping, talking
/mounting the odds as insurmountable

as history & fact degenerate,
replicate, fade into black

bagne, or, Criteria for Heaven

3. the ghost of Freda Capshaw

fr wendy agnew

    spirited, in every turn
streetcars practice diction
leaving toronto bloor street imprints
   vancouver electrical grids

combined centuries
    of longing
& vague impropriety
/1666, the year

the world, they told us, would end
       your love upon mine

    the following morning
    falling down the spiritual slide
in a long & unexpected

hangover

You still waiting for the Apocalypse? The millennium
came and went... the four-horsement were a no-show.
Your atom-bombshell stood you up, Woycheck!

Nah... it can't just run on like some never-ending
soap, goddamnit! There has to be some kinda finale.

    — issue #2, *2020 Visions*

rob mclennan

4. I can raise the dead

fr esta spalding

      a magnificent tremor of grief,
tumbling over stone
        & the collapsing shore

a price on every body, a mark
   curled on the face of cain

or spots of blood
     on the lazarus cloth
new testament of borrowed time

        in measured
frustration, she cries
     robot, the earth
       close this
    heart down for business
    & board up these broken windows

if it is impossible to feel, she says
it becomes impossible to hurt

bagne, or, Criteria for Heaven

5. unravelling another millennium of mystery

fr joe blades

      staring so far back the eyes bleed
/ten fingers & she loves me, loves me not
the painstaking tear of petals & stem

a resonance
     that constricts,
   breaks skin

as single eyes stare at the approaching ends
but not exactly what that entails

& new parents, hedging their bets, attend
     bible meetings, religious workshops

their newborn babys head
     sparkled clear
          w/ holy water

rob mclennan

6. turning and turning in the wide silent sky

fr amanda bielish

      & immersed
         in so many
common vowels
/icarus again, the singular
martyr & general falling star

      as buttons fly off my pinstriped 9 to 5
      new homes in my protective loincloth

the right agent would have found him an updraft
that storytelling action & lights out! bed...

bagne, or, Criteria for Heaven

7. the slight halt that rests in your words

fr dennis cooley

    a feeling & need for lustful things
/to break something
kill   shovelling
  fistfuls of earth over anger
to never let them see you...

    its the
    way that we learn
  to break ourselves
erase resolve & begin again, mean
    nothing & offend no-one

the tremble in your voice
    & a poem stressing everything
    & nothing at the same time

as i waited for the ground to open
, the skin, shuddering

as i waited for you
    to say something
but you never did

rob mclennan

8. hidden in its sheath of air

fr carla hartsfield

    where fire
rests upon rain, the realm
of steel over stone, carving
   radical design

   /this evening,
     as the days begin to blur
on edge,
   of marginalia
& where we sleep

& sand   creeps
into bedsheets

w/ an itch going nowhere
& a smile

& the descent of things not written
or yet entered into fact

bagne, or, Criteria for Heaven

9. salt of her primal sea

fr betsy struthers

     evoking something wilder
& more telling   dennis
  turning pages on bay street
poems dropping from his hands

she dreams of ocean
mountains rising from the earth

as craig drives sixteen hours
        to find her
& the taste of halifax harbour

even the police helicopters & radar
cant slow him down

rob mclennan

10. The Distances We Travel By Night

fr roy kiyooka

    there is nothing more important
than telling the story   engineering space
   between the ears
dreaming of children
or the reports of women

lapsed into comas & attacked
        raped & impregnated
delivering children during uninterrupted sleep
w/out an ounce of recognition
or pain

the distances
    we travel
your nostalgia moving
       a zeppelin
from home to work
& keys for locks that lose themselves
as lost as one could be
w/ catherine on her english throne
& her regular dreams

of horses

bagne, or, Criteria for Heaven

11. more in love with you than ever

fr bp nichol

      pot calling kettle black,
painting itself shades of red to keep hidden,
queens cards, busy brushing roses

   marking effects
out of causes, halting nothing
but all bets are off (so anything goes

'entering her bedchamber at night'
or so the storys told

maidens impregnated by all means
of demon, animal & fowl
lines so transparent

   altering
scripture & words
taking the words we speak & then

breaking them
/more than a means,
an end

rob mclennan

12. the skeleton of a little girl turning

fr jack spicer

      underneath the pavement
grave-markers of old
& over
      development
/first gone done
& digging w/ more permanent claws,
a carrion of tires

sympathy & walking spirits
      have holes in their shoes,
   dont go far
as subways burrow thru restful sleep

   excavation continues 3 storeys down
below your basement
& backyard pool   one history

on top of another one

13. I only shoot to kill

fr pj flaming

    straight from the iambic
        into something more
aiming to shoot
the magazine store that keeps porn shelved
    w/ the gun & sports magazines
the larger scope of narrative
  not a topography of invention
nor a deliberation of fools

when a man
    stalks a woman
      afraid to walk thru my neighbourhood
          in the heavy dark
female friends that stay
    on my couch
  until its light again

i only shoot
    to kill,
  she says,

& means it

rob mclennan

14. that was love but I kept on travelling

fr frank o'hara

      a week
   gone further into friday,
& one room no different than the rest
/craig still in ottawa dreaming of east water
   of airplane miles & a murder of crows

she looks out her window & she wonders,
     takes the initiative

building a young mans fantasy
       out of stone
a carrying place of rooms
& picture windows

& oh, what a view,
she says

bagne, or, Criteria for Heaven

15. here the rectangular sky opening up shh

fr patrick friesen

darker, then, a common age
       of insecurity & lost arts
         writing letters on a projected field
           of visions until theres
             nothing else
               the flicker

& spark of each day begun
     & done, assuming hemingways
         famous line, the sun
  to rise, the fade
& flare of old religion & the new dawn

    so much of the mind
begins w/ the earth, the proclaimed eternity
of months & rotation of vowels

& the expectation of another one
gaining or losing seconds every day
     to that final morning
        of giving in to fears
/of ice & the earth slowed cool

a floating frozen ball

rob mclennan

16. there are no divided hearts

fr maja bannerman

        there are no divided hearts,
    everything going
its own particular way
peg putting the al back in sexual
      or playing typewriter
          in a concept band
its all the same when you fall down laughing

  no matter what you complain,
     always returning to open emotional scars
& the four familiar walls
      strips of aorta toughen'd up
still sensitive from blood loss

    in a van hell bent to berekely
i want to drive until our fingers break
on the steering wheel
      & let all the smaller details
expose themselves

bagne, or, Criteria for Heaven

17. heard only the lament of crows

fr april bulmer

    thru the open window,
filling the purple-scented room
& keeping me awake again

  there is nothing further than the
truth, no destination
deep enough

    & spires that topple from churches
in the blur of hurricanes
& still a dozen people missing

  bruce quietly loving in jamaica
& craig, my favourite troubadour, writing songs,
& lamenting his east coast blues

as crows make their way
unhindered

rob mclennan

18. Perhaps the gods are returning

fr ted plantos

      arguments both for
    && against
a rational being that allows bosnia,
hiroshima
  (focussing on the negative),
allows collective memory loss
& whatever breaks out of the news today

      perhaps the gods, she breathes
living out our lives poetically, not narratively
as poets relate histories of the human heart
    & philosophers write novels
  on the millennium lyric

targeting every pop culture bullseye
& fears of a beginning or end

      & hesitation, once again, no more
*I love you*s on the radio

& listing all the darkness, bright

bagne, or, Criteria for Heaven

19. you paint snow falling

fr marilyn bowering

on branches
    where there is no snow
& children

against trees
where there are no trees

/it happens slowly
so we can not see it happening

small
   beautiful

snowflakes

rob mclennan

20. impossible love

fr maggie helwig

      your number one priority,
strange things indeed. in a hotel room
   two subways north,
     w/ an older woman, the sound
of waiting
in the bar downstairs, an old mans

     hacking & a television
        sporting kickboxing.
before the subways stops, i will.
ears over the future & green eyes
       over queen street,
  a young girls smile

& on the phone w/ impossible love
     in the belly of such a strange

city. i cant
   imagine anything else.

21. but you were always ambitious

fr margaret atwood

    though the real question is,
thirty years later w/ no place to go

re-defining everything
& placing a value on life & then poetry

a poem changes nothing else
except makes someone write another one

but you were always ambitious
wrote your name on envelopes & kept logs

all in the world remains singular
i want to call you on the telephone

two

bagne, or, Criteria for Heaven

i am again left with

my *own confusion* and the

momentary claritas the letters

enabled. was it ever more

than this — except the mind —

with equal insistence,

proposes an order — beyond all our

arguements

    — Roy Kiyooka

    ...once again, with my lacerated feet, [I] slipped into this sublime place where I was certain the supreme secret of the present, the past and the future resided...

        — Ahmed Jalal Erroumi, c. 1100 a.d.
         on the Great Pyramid of Cheops

rob mclennan

22. blowing a new day into a new season

fr lise downe

    never reaching the end,
miles of untended earth & fractured
   roman walls, the grander

human scale. letters written
never sent.

   for three hundred years they waited,
a line they dared anyone to cross

      but no one did. the disinterested
barbarian hordes
& the occasional hole poked thru stone hearth.

rebuilding the world
      from the roman eye
      in the centuries after christ, this empire

as hadrians wall, even fresh,
     not fifty years later,
sat unoccupied,

    grown over w/ weeds,
& grazing

bagne, or, Criteria for Heaven

And why regret the ocean's grieving ships?
Why lament the grandiose weather of stars?

— John B. Lee

rob mclennan

23. sadness becomes me

fr sina queyras

       stalking the pressure
          of the goose & the golden egg,
vanishing underneath petals
  of flesh
& gardens, one half
of the process of living, two people halved
      never equal a whole person
          / allowing grief
     to flow thru the body
not gnaw at the heart,
    a virus sadness becomes,

  she says. & she always does.
    scant pools filling w/ blue.
old virtues
such as pinching hard
     on the cheek
         instead of rouge,
small
& tireless. in the skin
     of a beautiful woman,

something that cant be removed.

bagne, or, Criteria for Heaven

24. the other eye the final hieroglyph

fr gwendolyn macewen

    when you know there are no bounds,
symbols etched in flesh the only record

  & what the first eye
      tends to forget,
images of the secular & the end
        of a sword, as sand dunes

    rise
     & fall
   w/ the same regularity
    & precision

whether we are here
or not. the other eye

   tracing a line between the sky
& the singular moon, digits
      of stars across the body
        of heaven,
bright tattoos. at the moment these things were written,
interpreting lines on sun-baked clay,
  calling

      i am here
      i am in this place

      now

rob mclennan

25. least of minstrels

fr tricia postle

      touching an arm, a
reassurance. marking the sounds
& distant figures,

living a dream of open doors
& strange affectations.
      you, left standing, a train
in the wrong direction

      from these houses
of correction, my fingertips
   worn numb from metal strings
& sketching the hands of angels.

after the fall, i held myself down

  & wandered east,
w/ a guitar case filled w/ brushes,
tubes of oil, old
paperback detective novels.

the unfinished sounds of music.

my days drinking coffee,
alone.

bagne, or, Criteria for Heaven

26. in the wake of spring

fr tracy brooks

   everything old
     is new again, old
adages, a time
of looking back. memoirs
  in the daily mail & winter warms,

the smell of oil from the furnace click.
in the wake of spring,
    the obvious,
     snow melts & dead animals, condom wrappers
     from the fall before
       & lone figures
loom on the periphery, joan
& the scent of burning flesh. or nostrodamus,
the prophet,

  in his hidden study, nearing
the end of his life, spirits
    from the weave of text
watching ancient volumes crumple ash.

   history, truly, is written by the victor.
   rewritten later by those
    who know how to hide a secret,
are smart enough to keep their mouths shut.

rob mclennan

27. like sunlight on the wings of birds

fr richard brautigan

      failing all else, i search
my pockets for change, the payphone
on the corner, still ringing

  & who
wants to answer it, we know
     the stories & hold
        our bodies back
     for the right practitioners

& its snowing here
     in the city & the sun is out
& i am drinking tea in unusual places
& she is miles away in a car
       doing
     whatever it is she does
     but i know she is doing it well

bagne, or, Criteria for Heaven

28. into remarkable clouds

fr steven heighton

      the persistence & knowledge
of the 20th century. nothing lasts forever,
a lesson
   i learn.
grasping at abstracts
       & a handful of straws, write me
          a poem, she says,

about angels. & tossing them far
into electrical space, how much
       is enough
pop songs w/ broken wings
   & television pulp
w/ religious & end-of-the-world
         overtones. *free*

as a word, she croons. that bird.
   these wings
she gives me

cant lift me nearly high enough.

rob mclennan

29. winter when our minds fill up with snow

fr dennis cooley

      until were nearly obsessed with it
attitudes are inflexible things
   tight   on the cusp

suzanna moodie in a house somewhere north
far more north then,
     even if it were here

      as buildings creep higher
          towards polar north
& bulldozers plough an eager path

the city of boston shut down
     at least once a year
     by the first hint of blowing snow

      ah, you silly americans, cold chorus

even as we cross wires, wrap our
     minds around sled dogs
       & pierre burton,
sergeant whatsisname of the mounted police,

     two months in twelve of bad skiing

bagne, or, Criteria for Heaven

30. sharp as stainless steel

fr carolyn zonailo

     in the hands of silent muses,
wandering uneven montreal streets. when words
turn into glass, a sharpness
that almost bleeds   & as clear
   as photographs at bens, walls
      & ceilings of famous her & them, faces
& sandwiches

      there is a clarity here
that is easily missed,
     from the heads of pins
& unconnected dots. throwing muses,
not saints, into the centre ring
beside boxes of recent books
& a sony outlet on ste catherines st
beside orders of hooded monks
& beckett, three years
    between the holy man
& the skeletal myth. intangible reasons
      that make anyone do

      fate or religion

& forget purity,
that intolerable fiction

as even medieval bands
sold the bodies of their catholic saints
to churches
bone by charred bone

rob mclennan

31. and how we slowly began to look like her

fr linda rogers

      in the southern states,
the mirror'd hull
   of a government box
discolours in the form
of the virgin mary,
arcs
of oil & water
     nearly three storeys tall

      hundreds of believers appear
to pay homage,
pray
  as psychic hotlines go under
         in quebec & elsewhere
when no one saw it coming
the incredible jojo savard

     who says religion
         is a fading negative,
different articles of belief
  moving tenuous into the future, imperfect
        & unknown
& the desperation to find something
     to hold on to
      images of worry beads & other artifacts
        so it must be true

bagne, or, Criteria for Heaven

32. with dark coming on and the cold

fr august kleinzahler

      dancing like the sky is falling,
like its 1999

      catching the quill of myth,
about understanding the present,
not the future

      where everything is old,
            descended from breathing
& tributaries arranged into a lattice
of imaginary gardens

      of alice & christopher robin
      holding hands & rushing old oak doors,
water-shrunk & forcing their way
    thru keyholes,
    & dreams of keyholes

         waking up when theyre nearly thirty
         married & held down
           by mortgage
         the rest of their lives

    going back to sleep again

rob mclennan

33. giddy during the earthquake

fr john barlow

      like the cow that burnt down chicago,
a tremor of earth on the ontario tip,
one part a domino on another. one half
           of her mothers house, rattling
                       glass
& a process of confusion
     that her mother never felt,
one floor below on the other side.

its snowing in vancouver but not in ontario,
               things
      we arent used to, shaking routine
      like monday night football on a thursday
      or canandian terrorists. a bomb goes off

today in paris & no one
     even blinks. it fits
         w/ the way the mechanism turns, pools
         of expectation & relief

that its them not us. smooth
& nearly cooled. sometimes silence
     is more terrifying than gunshot,
      a hush in the air before something begins,
        or maybe if something ever

really did, we would
     shake apart, w/ nervous

& screeching laughter

bagne, or, Criteria for Heaven

34. how tired the ashes are. what weight in a rose?

fr patrick lane

     the cities, they say, built
on the bones of the dead. now

     you are sleeping, & lone trucks
rattle your bedroom window. where

     did you come from? i ask.
but you never answer.

     you asked me once, but i had
already forgotten. moved. & faint

     the taste of ashes in my
mouth, the imperceptible night. these

     four walls holding & the
weightless moon, leaving almost

         the faintest scar.

rob mclennan

35. japan in my own language

fr karen maccormack

     misunderstanding the dance,
the two step of honour, the rise of ambitions,
of we who are about to die —

clouding over fragments of human nature
filaments burning as they flame
& everything else the taste of smoke

two scottish women over coffee
deconstruct the japanese perspective
from 1940 onwards
old enough to be young
   during wwII
& missing out on their own eyes gloss

ive heard tell
    that westerners
can never comprehend buddhism
to truly understand
you have to be born
into it

   like monty python
to the french
a joke
you can never
explain

36. how little a dead person bleeds

fr sylvia legris

      tying up an arrangement of flowers,
a staccato gesture in worn silk

the days of the active monarch
      /births & deaths
    & regents turning tides

      of succession & starting over
every new death marking
      a beginning in the realm
        of months

dating back time to borders in sand,
where continuity fails

    & memory is vocal
    & only endures five minutes

      or as far as one thinks,
fifty years of our regent queen, of
    standing

rob mclennan

37. Those indelible blue solitudes

fr george mcwhirter

        standing at once
in the rural snow, mirrors
& slush, further
    into that blue night

        as newsprint covers the west
w/ grey, layers on victoria
stopping progress & snowploughs
   relays
      of beginnings
brought about before them

        on page five, guns
            are carefully cocked,
& films shine casually
on the scent of evil
    held safely in the past

   in blue white toques, closing
       the book on another year,
          I dont
eat fire I speak it   building puzzles
out of so many mismatched pieces

     turning hope to despair
       to hope again

bagne, or, Criteria for Heaven

38. peddling clouds like bicycles

fr roger nash

      in ottawa today,
false january spring
         deceptively warm & fluttering snow
           so going out for coffee
             on the safe side,
               picking supplies

         where a coffee staff
            working the previous, a jab
           in her calf
        as she removes the trash
a used needle poking thru plastic bag

        as she sits, pumped
          w/ medication
      & worry, off till friday
hospital finding traces of heroin
    the quickest flash of highs

& lows   of knowing & not

clouds rolling over like pedestrians
      & later on a grey carpet
         keeping us down w/ a cool & quiet moisture,
             new flakes

    w/ only the faintest outline

rob mclennan

39. the melancholy tango of the rain

fr stephen scobie

       its easy to assign significance,
an eye
   in every corner
or foot on familiar terms. driving

   thru a music of trees,
         no house
            nor human eye for hours. in england,
where space is rare, fragments of the countryside
   remain open, to remind the future

   that such sights exist, building london up
a tower'd babel,
to heavens clouds.

        in central asia,
      the nomads still wander
         along paths 800 years wide,
   when genghis was khan
     leading flocks of sheep

     past piles of bones from ancient massacres,
         a second nature
            of calloused hands,
        the yellow sun,

    the single rise to blue

bagne, or, Criteria for Heaven

40. The other side, the mountain gag

fr stacy doris

    burying their dead their usual way,
what exactly that means

        the ancient romans
            leaving little in the way
of human artifice, no face

            but the painted shale, blowing
                  chunks from the peak
            of pompeii, an instant
                of historical grace

        ad 79, one day
            in august, as two cities
                were swept
                    under forty feet of ash
& bodies frozen where they stood

    soldiers on the beach grabbling handfuls of sand
        & slave girls clutching children,
            mouths open wide in hysteria

            the long human shadow,
        smoke clouds carbonising bread, wood
            the extent of modern wisdom,

                putting out a thin finger

rob mclennan

41. as if life could touch its metaphors

fr nicole brossard

    sliding, slanted roof
    pushing fever to its highest

       & becoming (politically) incorrect
       as the lights are dimmed
       & watching from this side of it

the simpson case turning culture on its ear
/of race & hero worship

five years ago & whoda thunk
a civil case in millions, now in rerun

    thinking in terms of black-and-white
    we interrupt this presidential debate
    this seinfeld episode half-lost already

oh to step back america into old pepsi commercials
get tossed a famous jersey w/ a scent of accomplishment

bagne, or, Criteria for Heaven

42. to follow the frightening shape of their desires

fr john newlove

>   the shape
> of the long-necked pharoah,
>   akhenaten, the heretic
> in the midst of contemporary anyones
> & *the new chronologie*
>
>   he who displaced the pantheon
>   of egyptian gods
>   for the disc of the sun, the single
>   aten
>
>   as saul chased david
>   across the holy land,
>   akhenaten incurring the wrath of priests
>
>   who would erase his name from temples
>   & the official story,
>   before his body
>   was bone, dry
>   in the sanddunes
>
>   making fodder for wolves
>   & interpretation,
>   lost idols returning to pedestals
>
>   the forging of a point of view
>
>   the raising of two hands

rob mclennan

43. & revenge w/ the speed of light

fr mark cochrane

        what you want to see
you will   slapping
your thigh like blood
    on glass,
        mirrors
         enter strangely here

  w/ the honesty
       of hurt, she cuts ties
completely (& leaves

the space of the poem) there is
    no room
to argue   no slip

that hasnt already been attempted,
       documenting
failures until

    mouths have closed
 & cups
   overflowed

, a face
of pale skin

bagne, or, Criteria for Heaven

44. Everything open gets filled, gets closed.

fr ronna bloom

quiet
& quiet

because you know

what darkness
means

rob mclennan

45. there are no rules anymore

fr darren wershler-henry

                    stalking the craft
                in a clearing of breath
the absence of lines
erase
    composure, the mother&father-lode
of inventiveness   the growing yawn

between sparks of alternate light. it speaks
                to us in ages, in bounds.

where once our hands were busy,
            banging stones into music
        or rolling out art on construction paper.
scizzors. glue. things written
in a concrete cage, castles & landscapes
                made out of clay
    & acts

    of imagination.
            not even mole hills out of rough earth.

bagne, or, Criteria for Heaven

46. shards, fragments, detritus

fr david arnason

      where this is going I dont know,
    in my head all over
      only what I see on the horizon
        & race toward

hurtling in directions that cant be slowed
cloning sheep & lower sperm counts in white males
maybe a hundred years from now we are all replicated

or as photocopies as the toner downs,
    further away from the original
      being canadian, that inherent racism
      we all have but do not talk about
  I just keep quiet   the hand

      moving quicker than the eye, the fear
        rising quicker than the mind,

    jumping at shadows, slowly learning
        all this out of me

a few less white people cant be bad
/this is not a poem on intent

rob mclennan

47. looking for what has been lost

fr michael crummey

      trying to grasp
          a sense of the world, whole,
prague churches older than this sense of ourselves

    st raphaels in glengarry county
a church & community transplanted scotland
to ontario indian lands, 1870s
          the oldest church ruins
      in all these north americas

      or figuring a timeline,
    what was going on that day,
        a breath of continuity

if george vancouver was still shipping out the west coast
& napoleon w/ his sticky hands on thrones,
the mayan calendar as precise to the second

& romans? what romans? even napoleon
wouldnt discover ancient egypt
for another thirty long radical years

bagne, or, Criteria for Heaven

48. they lie with me in a common grave

fr patrick lane

>   six-year-old beauty queen
>   found strangled in a basement
>   like a childs
>   discarded doll

> so much for a career in modelling
> & everybody loves a winner
>   — once theyre dead —

as old blue eyes sinatra fights bad health & heartache,
his record company preparing,
        post-mortem, pre-release

>   in the wake of resurgance after his departure
>   but hes gotta make the initial step

>   or the porn movie clip called norma jean
>   where does it end, the stuff
>   of executive dreams
>   get your wallets ready, the toll-free
>   number, catch it

rob mclennan

49. things do happen emma laraine's daughter smiling due november

fr sharon thesen

      & forgetting sometimes how the world
          is filled
       w/ people, left & right, each
           a story
barely told
     johns son,
  neil, not a year old, caring
         little for such talk
      & gossip, but laughing
       at my twitching
        fingers

  70s icon andy kaufman,
tying busboy apron on
     after taxi tapings, his 2nd job

  to keep his bases covered,
as regular guy to keep his head on straight,
     a foothold in the real

     & filling then this
payphone gaunt w/ quarters
      once john leaves

    & my daughter
    says hello

bagne, or, Criteria for Heaven

50. the sound of our own steps over the high green meadows

fr kim maltman

       tracing a path
     out of greenery & maps,
          the smell
of recognition & the fragile past. the grass
        is ever greener,

        driving thru suburbs or the rain,
          to see where knees
            were routinely skinned,
spaces overcome w/ housing clones,
departmart store where you once played ball

     twice, to reminisce,
     a field of open yards
        & crabapple trees
     taken over by a sprawling burb
that could be anywhere, toronto ottawa chicago

   of ten year old fingers
     around hard fruit
        capable of bruises
     & broken windows

  & what became of you, once you hit something

rob mclennan

51. We are deep in the centre, fixed and very slow

fr sophia kaszuha

        the psychology of killers,
    a fenceline on both love & hate

of the kidnapped who fall in love
w/ the 'nappers,
    the intimate knowledge
  of small dark places,
of the goings-on between two bodies

"gold & love affairs
    are difficult to hide"
      we cant all live forever but parts do

        john turns 50, rusty gets a haircut
        neil laughs & laughs & waves his hands
            at everyone

    nearly a year old & for all we know
    enjoying a joke that the rest of us dont get

bagne, or, Criteria for Heaven

52. a place lighted only by your eyes

fr nain nomez

       talking into a heritage,
a shifting reference point

     where she falls again,
   briefly into the poem,
           two voices
overlapping, speaking
  in a higher tone

       the antiquities of the past
         should stay there,
    she speaks, a british accent
          taking at face value

    gone is gone
       is gone again
    every new day
        starting over
        starting over
      talking into a heritage
this poem collapsing
    into itself
a shifting reference point
   she — speaks,
    a quiet
   stellar place

rob mclennan

53. I do not think I am thinking

fr robin blaser

>   interfering w/ our need to know,
>   the space of the individual
>
>   kid pelts a snowball
>   at the back of my head,
>   takes a
>   picture & sells it to *Hard Copy*,
>   tells all his friends
>
>   the embarrassment
>   of the local scribbler, walking w/ arrogance
>   & bags of paper
>
>   the unfocussed
>   frustration
>   of the neighbourhood children
>
>   little buggers —
>   six months from now
>   Ill steal their bikes
>   while theyre asleep
>
>   & throw them in the river
>   maybe get a poem out of it
>   maybe get an
>
>   article about me in a newspaper

54. that these songs go unfinished

fr barry mckinnon

     vancouver transit
        thru a bc wilderness
       stanley park
          & visions of delsing

  (the unsettling quiet
    of the west,
  all electric)

      in memory,
     everything set
     to music, even if
        the facts grow cloudy

    bits of phrases trappt beneath the skull
     & half-remembered songs,
      a soundtrack
     & this weary life

what exists
   w/in the unconscious mind,
     a relay switch
    to trigger pulses,
      or

     (repeat & fade...)

rob mclennan

55. he says a name for water

fr maria erskine

      raining ice in the february dawn
as power fades from my outer limbs
& they shut down lebreton flats
   the ache   of polar caps

everybody leaves a mark
somehow
you have to know how to look

her fine freckled arms
at the back of my neck
traced, years later

  or amelia earhart
decades after disappearing
, a right-sized shoe
found
on a south pacific island

       washed above
& ashore a rim of years
& forgetfulness,
the memory never far from gone

   & appearing almost suddenly
   & fervent

a diamond

showing thru

56. did his magic for him, suddenly

fr michelle desberats

      as julian the magician raised his hands
& coffee appeared in toronto shops

    the popularity of all this death,
& lurking poets who cant get arrested

    but never for lack of trying
/an article on writers & suicide notes

      or kurt cobain,
      listeners calling his chaos beautiful,
      & encapsulating youth

hindsight 20-20
    & when he sang that he was fucked up

everyone cheered

rob mclennan

57. waiting for a rescue hours overdue

fr carmine starnino

    even buddhists
        have to come in
      from the rain,
          she says

58. Made by her passage through the open lanes

fr e. j. pratt

      darkness
    & darkness. the equal space
        shared
            by every north american
city. stripmalls
& movie stalls. roots
      crawling surface still,
infecting all that stands in its path.

    what was admired abroad,
from the offset, not the corporations,
        the structure of ideologies
            or government
but those american
      cities
  large
      & overwhelming. awe-inspiring,

  towering structures
almost of greek or roman equivalent
in our present hour. almost, now,
        a thing gone mad.

            to be seen for miles,
absorbing all light.

rob mclennan

59. Be in danger. Look

fr yves troendle

three

I tell myself when I am well I won't love you anymore.

— D.C. Reid

bagne, or, Criteria for Heaven

Dear, dear! How queer everything is to-day! And yesterday things went on just as usual. I wonder if I've changed in the night? Let me think: was I the same when I got up this morning? I almost think I can remember feeling a little different. But if I'm not the same, the next question is: Who in the world am I? Ah, that's the great puzzle!
— *Alice in Wonderland*, Lewis Carroll

Tuesday, 10 June 1997

Pisces (Feb. 19-March 20): You'll be intoning, "What goes around comes around!" You might be asking, "Is this deja vu?" Scenario features familiar places, faces. Romantic liason lends spice — protect yourself in clinches.

rob mclennan

60. and it's like someone escaping that we run to mere breathing

fr dionne brand

        thirty seconds
            from a doomsday hour,
    the smell & vagueness of ticking

having my nightmares now
while im awake, a wall of fire
      over the horizon
           or my daughter disappeared
        from her nepean
           playground

      sudden solar flares
           turning worlds end
      & the single commodity

        a stray value placed
      before snuffed
        not after

midnight   & i want
  to hold you in my arms already
& i am dialing as i speak

      & running

bagne, or, Criteria for Heaven

61. you and the portrait that I see

fr sean david ross

     a shade of black
& multiple television screens. image
is everything, nothing, everybody says so.
          drink product
          eat product
          & live happy, get girls.

    simplifying resolution to the optic nerve,
          not the lone alcoholic
                swatting his wife
or putting pins to his wrists,
but the young pretty models in swimwear
  who hand over popular drinks, please please me.

    as everything we see is something else, ice cubes
    filled w/ demons amid ravaged beauties.

    i fall for another waitress
        in a logical arc, the slip
            of subservience & smiling,
    wispy abstracts of comfort
        & reliability.
tell me what it is
tell me what it is
        i want another
    t-shirt, cigarette, lite beer. buy one,
        get one.

still sizing a body by the position of its logo.
these days, even trends are no longer fashionable.

62. like the waving handkerchiefs of kings

fr john b. lee

   to put one swell of ink to linen,
tales both mysterious
& immense

       if i had a nickel for every time i died,
       she writes, id still feel dead inside

          cutting a foothold off, a sigh,
          the scent
             of former tenants, small prints

when the english arrived, native
north american cities held their thousands
& their tens of thousands

   devastated by disease, smallpox
& others hacking limbs, the movement
of the earth beneath them

       & reduced to splinters
          once
            the europeans turned to look

   centuries later, british men take pictures
built by thoughtless hands, grey owl

telling stories to keep the spirit
sane, a feather

       in his felt hat

After 46 days in the psycho
ward, I have learned not to laugh
when no one else is laughing.

  — Daniel Jones

 It takes guts to know some happiness
& not make a poem of it.

  — Daniel Jones

rob mclennan

63. sorrow side

fr jacqueline larson

        snow arriving gently on all sides,
        freezing rain & spring lionizing,
        marching in, marching out

even when you dont want to see it,
wake up tomorrow & yr dead

        oh to believe in something anything
        heavens grip
        picking children from their beds
        for grand & unknown purposes

    , the gentle beating of angel wings

        53% of americans
        still believe in their existence

even more claim that elvis is still alive

& thats presley not stoiko,
        skating clear paths
        thru fame & product endorsement

slipping easily to the quick & more banal

i refuse to believe this is all accidental

bagne, or, Criteria for Heaven

64. i'll get on the next ferry when it reaches me."

fr janet charman

        modern prophets
  who lead their spirits to the next life,
    to arrive on other planets,
        an alien ship beyond the comet hale-bopp,

        signals for an end of civilisation,
        religious confusion
        & a penchant for crossdressing

a woman in california,
repeated visions of an america not long
, buried one-third under a weight of flood

    i never see this stuff on CNN
    this two millennia worth of doomsday
    rain of fire, earth & wind

& needing to know, before i go

        if we had six hours left to live,
        would you call me

      , would you

rob mclennan

65. away into the dark lake forever

fr tom marshall

    this is where i describe
  post-mortem / thigh-high
      on a quivering edge

inflate the structure of a distant past
to hook w/out pining or pulsing sentiment
i do not know & i do not know already

    satellites over the city bypass
      glowing twilight
        & dust
  where this window may as well
    have bars / the do-or-die
      mythology

death & taxes
or exchanging christmas cards
in june

    if you care to look,
this is where youll find me

      : in a whole lotta space
    adjoining doubt

    & the particulars of grace

& not believing anything
, even the things that can be plucked

bagne, or, Criteria for Heaven

66. The moon is a tear caught by a tongue

fr natalee caple

      at the final break,
           finding belief where before was none,
the real power hidden
   behind parlour tricks
   & the occasional sleight-of-hand

to be here in the morning
for you to read this,
      almost to expect due closure

to disappoint between the gut & tongue
the grand human ego, that we
     are the only voices speaking
  , that we personally
         would see apocalypse

schoolkids under 1950s desks
   when the big one swooned, Miss Atom
      Bombshell winking back,
         the biggest tease in the modern world

   /& where you might read as teardrop
i read rip, a small
torn scrap
   or scar

turning on another one

rob mclennan

67. weaving their invisible ways

fr andrew stubbs

>every movement forward a hold
>in a larger quest for answers
>, not questions

>i do my best work in solitude,
>the finest movement after dark

>agnes in church every morning for prayer,
>afterward an affirmation of tea
>& muffin

>each a soluble mark to single quest
>tho sometimes
>not as deliberate
>or informed

reincarnated kings & queens making tabloids,
running out of people to be reborn

>there has to be more
to this series of distractions

& doctrine

bagne, or, Criteria for Heaven

68. for you just two steps short of the measure

fr michelle leggott

    holding water & watering holes,
        a window of figures walking
      w/ fewer clothes,
    in the wake of available spring

marvelling at my choice of popular medium,
a drink in the royal oak among friends

    outside the strip club,
    the wandering protester, The Wages
      Of Sin
        & voices thrown in after him,
arrows pooling the pedestrian crowd

    every time the teevee blinks
      its something
a few dozen bodies in a suicide clot
governments stealing our collective breath
or picking up a gun somewhere & shooting

    spending more of my time asleep
or another drink

rob mclennan

69. In your painting, it's a soundless dark space

fr michael redhill

    hard to look past physical presence.
hadrians palace shadowing long over rome

    time as eroding & healing touch
easing caligulas madness thru the things he built

      not everything
        is as easy,
  what faces i have seen, she writes

& cleopatra, the last pharaoh, losing
heart & a position in space

  pinnacling her portrait in a wealth of film,
sixty years of american cinema

each new word having the final say

bagne, or, Criteria for Heaven

70. possibility in this place, in your body, here.

fr maggie helwig

    more possibility than you would care
        to admit,

otherwise.   the tug of gravity
    & ego. a snowballs

chance in hell. winding

our western ways, the frame of mind
    that sees only
our own accomplishments, claiming as far along
    as the body goes,

    more often than not, the shortest distances
between two points, a straight line.
    or freuds, "sometimes a cigar
        is only a cigar"
            new books claiming

an alien intervention in the ancient world, egyptian
    pyramids or the aztek temples,
        old hands that couldnt
            have done for themselves.

the limitations of a point of view.

    where we would write a thesis on the matter,
    add layers,
        ancient simplicity
            a single step,

saying, here,

    this is how its done.

rob mclennan

71. He's had it up to here.

fr clint burnham

    as the reader reads,
darkness over age & romantic drift,
        already sick of angels

    & premonition. those close to their own death,
      he claims, have the ability
          to see spirits.
nothing gained w/out a price.

hiding bodies in plain view, teethmarks
      ravage new orleans flesh
    & wisdom sleeps in comic books.

never is this glamour w/out substance.
slipping trade secrets in poetry books,

        places no one would think to look.

bagne, or, Criteria for Heaven

72. to sew in her tongue

fr anne kelly

    phrasing a further point,
        the unexamined life
& socrates embracing a bowl of hemlock

      "once upon a time
          in America," she reads
    a pot of fine melting
until a thick white paste

      "once upon a time"
    turning tales out of class
    where the wolf
        between three pigs
      & riding hood
    bleed formless
        & indistinguishable

& were only there to stereotype a part

as my jewish friend martin shakes his head,
    their calendar year
      in the 4700s,

seeing all this time-specific heartache
    as a formal
    posture

rob mclennan

73. like a moon among all these things

fr don coles

        a saying
           from the land of nod,
        where cain disappeared to
            — a name for sleeping

if you die by your own hand,
you return as a little bird, perhaps a raven
    if ever you return at all

        today i have marks on my forearms
          , an unfamiliar script
that none of my friends can read
& i dont know how they got there

        a flock of blackbirds
    blanket the diminishing sun
      , circles on a haze of concrete
          & the effects of gunshot

on a rideau centre floor, a teenager
drops down to his knees
  , weeps blood

        already my legs & arms begin to swell

        already i carry too many keys
        for doors i will no longer open

four

They will come on wings of steam, the young citizens of America will fly through the air, across the great ocean, to visit old Europe. They will come to see the monuments of bygone ages, the ruins of the great cities, just as we today visit Southeast Asia to stare at the crumbling glories of the past.

Thousands of years hence, they will come.

— *The Millennium*, Hans Christian Anderson
trans. Erik Christian Haugaard

bagne, or, Criteria for Heaven

74. you must make to survive.

fr suzanne buffam

        as long fingers write
from a greek island,
    there are
        no constants. still we build,
        & certain artifacts crumble at a touch.

       i am holding my head
          in this worried gaze, new hairs
             sparkle grey, certain bones
               & joints begin to ache.
i help my dentist build attachments on his house.

what i have loved, i have loved
    fully, well. make concessions

       for abstracts, the hearth. stepping
          around other peoples human constructs.

       when my grandfather was young,
          building a fence between neighbours
       that now
new trees & growth make obsolete.
green earth reclaiming pockets of land.

    not even this is constant.

rob mclennan

75. where silent, unrefractive whiteness lies.

fr p.k. page

        in a sheen of canadian white
   larger than the scope of years, national
           rather than international

here i am sweating
   in the earths coldest capital, learning
            my own limits
& biases, an obsession
w/ snow
   & place. watching an irish history
        of baseball, a backdrop
        of bone crushing blows, or scotlands

        decision for independence,
their first clean breath

in three centuries. some things
   are base, basic, defining

   lies & lines in a foundation.
      now

      see there, not victim
      nor victor, but built

     upon living in a physical landscape,
     moving to a place & taking over,

     taking. pioneer years. just now,
     learning in the end what the cost.

bagne, or, Criteria for Heaven

76. The name is the bullet.

fr anne le dressay

    what becomes inevitable,
the death of someone famous,
& everything
  changes.

    such a public outpouring of grief,
      for someone that they never knew, photos
        in tabloids, reports
          on the cbc, the wheelchair'd grandmother

    who once shook her hand.
youre very welcome, the grandmother said,
& the crowd after got a good chuckle out of it.

again, to see it coming. what price
fame, & how much

    were willing to pay.
the name is the bullet. i fire regularly
      & at random. ripples

& skipping stones. after all this bluster,
      the water surface smooth

    & undisturbed.

rob mclennan

77. secretly more for himself than his reader

fr andrew steeves

    what some moments are meant to be
/in ottawa south, my grandmother
losing bits of her eighty years, yelling
    my hellos from a few feet away

this day is family again, despite months
    of inactivity & silence, thin
    wires tugging at sentiment
      & the lower intestine

    around my uncles kitchen,
      kate plays w/ cousins
  she hasnt seen in four years, laughing
    around chairs & bushes

      & thats two-thirds of her life so far,
      a long time
      for anyone

bagne, or, Criteria for Heaven

78. is burning burning burning burning up.

fr douglas brown

    poems centred on the apocalypse,
        bookshelf full,
    this century begins to crumble

    the inconsistencies of belief,
      so few of current new
        & old testaments
      painting angels
lost in books removed, the book
of enoch, firstborn son
    of cain

as nostrodamus spied ahead to the 37th century,
leagues away, not just
    current fire & brimstone lore

what does this tell you,
even if you are listening,
    taking that risk

    dont come over now, she says
        on the digital end
    maybe tomorrow

    ill still be here

rob mclennan

79. and am nearing home

fr robin skelton

>   fixated on sounds
>   & cultural marks,
>   "run with scizzors"
>
>   or bus stop graffiti telling stories
>   almost unheard. two women
>
>   wear the same green dress
>   & share the no. 7 bus. who says
>   that variety
>
>   is a desired spice? even if
>   your tongue was cinnamon,
>
>   she writes, skin
>   were honey. this is
>   a singular turn,

& i am nearing home, dear reader,
    skimming. i am
recognising familiar marks.

bagne, or, Criteria for Heaven

80. means what it does not, and more's the pity

fr heather spears

        into a great debate
          & widening
    the fiery fall of lucifer morningstar from grace

      writing *fall* not *plunge*, how it is read
        as tho he might have tripped
         on a tree root or a stone

to never again enter the silver city
this poem beginning to believe its own mythology

            saying, one slip & you are
            outta there

         or a story
from the far east, of an atheist
  so sure of the non-existence
      of god
    he repeated it constantly thru his life

        stepping inadvertently into it,
           a criteria for heaven,
        holding the idea of god
              in his permanent thots

& dying, he was fooled again,
            not a bit of this making
        too much sense

      tho it doesnt matter what i have seen
      you wouldnt believe me if i told you anyway

rob mclennan

81. the perfect ending to their perfectly ordinary evening.

fr jamie reid

        takes her guitar out & sings.
        exactly where she needs to be.

pennywhistle, bongos, spoons. butterfly
    lands on the back deck.

        says something, says, says something.
        catch my eye, a woman
            walking by
        in shorts.

thank you tomorrows news, as a poet
        hes got nice hair. the airport
bookstore carries more of me
            than i do.

bagne, or, Criteria for Heaven

82. and the sun keeps coming...

fr m. travis lane

      (where do you want it?)

  proof of the biblical flood
        six millennia before christ,
  a water line burning the middle east

        moving an itch
      along the tongue,

      come undone,
  raining palms against rough skin

  taking note of a winter or a summers day
    not noticing the freshness, cool
      similarities of blue

    things to do & not to do
    you are here & you are
      never here

wheres mike hammer when these mysteries begin?
lines so sharp, embedded in skin

rob mclennan

83. for a little linseed oil and a chamois

fr nancy bullis

    who wouldnt want return,
  a safety into someones arms

        the star wars drag,
      a theory of disjointedness
          /an unfinished story
         defining
      a particular generation

    & oldest good & evil shows
     or natural disaster films
        reminding us how small we are
           /a little linseed oil

      the less we know the happier we are
comforting dark, almost waiting
  for the information age   to finish
       unaffected by the particulars of change

bagne, or, Criteria for Heaven

84. to the portal? Advance still backwards yet more?

fr gerry shikatani

       like chickens w/ their heads chopped, .
  bloodshot & running circles

do you still, call out my name
finding trace outlines
  in a former lovers prose
gleeful i left such full effect

       or watching _____ _____
     on a thursday, turning & telling,
    you had better not
    put this into a poem, & i know
    he means it

hard to continue
    on this apparent uselessness of poems
as i go around spouting them
& certainly not a new idea

as death lands casually in ottawa
the poet not the hooded scythe
& says he may never write again
even tho he will

rob mclennan

85. In the distance there is the distance.

fr jeff meyers

    where most fears are brought to light

& land close

    take from me a space,
to work technologies
from one hand
down

    a fisherman off the coast
of peru, weaving nets
& collecting his catch the way his
      forebears did, eighteen
  centuries of remembering

      one generation down,
          & my daughter
only knows the city, streetlights
that burn out stars, the accumulation

of 150 eastern ontario turns,

        skipping sidewalk rope
     & asphalt tag

        one more sign
     to step away

bagne, or, Criteria for Heaven

86. in my lonely house, I'm drunk with passion again

fr constantine cavafy

    whirling dirvishly
        around visions of worlds end,
a pawn of old stories

gleaning new days
  from the rubble of the old, ages speaking
      in broken promises

        of ragnarok,
          & other explosive doors.
    build it?

    she asks, its built.
    noahs ark hanging high & dry,
    prospero w/ neither kingdom nor wisdom to toss.

      an island
      impossible
        to leave.

rob mclennan

87. in secret places I hide my fat and wait for rain for rain for rain

fr clare latremouille

secret places i am thinking of,
    a cafe on victoria street watching biker gangs
        in the british columbia interior

            sticking one foot out & then another
      marking a change of seasons
          & remorse

          throw up your hands
              & i can catch you
        few things here are beyond redemption

you make your bed & then you leave it
set the orchestra pit on fire & watch it burn

              turning tail again
                    once the snow flies

    under layers of winter
    & salt

bagne, or, Criteria for Heaven

88. your shame, white veil, or the peace of God.

fr lara aase

      fine tuning regiments of place,
tell me where you are, i cannot
  see you. images of mary cropping up
      for christians everywhere, america
          & europe, the holy
virgin tour. secular images
  rise along the skin of my arms
       & chest.
& whole groups sing out, save me, save me.
i fall into your prayers & sigh,
    similar lungs & a new salvation.

      scriptures only hint at love.
        oiling the dusty feet of christ

w/ her long brown hair,
   ive never been religious, she says, but i
     know what i like.
mother theresa, saint or albanian whore.

this is a car poem.
i always write about cars when im
       in the south.

rob mclennan

89. I will know from the inside out

fr anne le dressay

    if you hold it right,
      they tell me,
    something about the proper tool

every saint is a weapon,
    the falls of lourdes or karnac stones,
     back 6000 years
       of carbon dating

     even technology
       a version
    of events, a familiar tale, a man
      finding electrical fields

& healing touch
    amid pillars of stone   too much,

    in maps of ancient skies, what
    we will ever know, i cant

    imagine   the only thing
i know for sure, a french speaking woman
  in the twentieth century, pulls off
    her sweater &
     forgets it
      on a nearby chair

   ill hold it for her, here,
until she gets back

bagne, or, Criteria for Heaven

90. the silence — my stories are of no consequence

fr stuart ross

      a cigarette
          lands on the floor & the heel
of a shoe pushes into it. an orange spark
    disintegrates
       where there is no other light.

         pick up
      on what is happening, this is
        a slowness, home
          stretch, an
       intermission of sorts.

even the pauses themselves are pregnant
        /if this
were a film, this scene

          would be the darkness,
      the trenchcoat man waiting
          for his payoff
        or defeat,

         the five minutes
     before the stoolie gets it,
what everyone around was expecting,
    but somehow
      still
    managing to suspend
   until you, too, jump.

rob mclennan

91. waiting and waiting to finish what she started.

fr nathalie stephens

      hands do what hands do & we
    go on, opening the pandoras box,
she reads, pandoras curiosity
getting on w/ the best of her.

   if this were any other, would the
story have been different, days when
        certain times of the lunar cycle
  frightened village men, leaving young girls
         alone in dark tents
    to bleed until spirits dried.

  & now you tell me, prying the lid & all the
        evils of the world set loose, pandoras
sexual innuendo or bluebeards egg, the women

      who cant let sleeping
    dogs, the best of them & sometimes
    winning in the end & sometimes
        losing.

see how all the evils of the world & what
        do you see when you hold the
         mirror still, what
      do you, entering
  here & going

      i see nothing, she purrs, but already
        her eye flickers left &
          mind
        begins to swirl.

92. the dream dreaming itself out of control.

fr stan rogal

      back to where i thot i was
        before, she too,
unsure if she left at all. the longer we seem to go,
      the further back we think we

      started. in darwins lifetime,
      pointing the creation of the world
    to 4000 b.c.,

   a morning in october. now, they think
        the sphinx alone
      nearly twice that age, mere a teen
          when others said adam & eve
         lifted fig leaves
         to their newness
            & begat, begat.

today i know where i am
  & where you are, two lines
     that rarely intersect. i dream
        living years
         going on
      before opening my eyes.

     dreaming years beyond reconstruction.

rob mclennan

93. the small pieces of her go.

fr shannon braemer

    skin beginning to white & flake,
        the dry cold of the seasons turn,
& an opposing point of view.

this has always been about something, sometimes
   her & then myself, she
an itch behind my eyes

    i cant scratch out.
        icarus had his own day in the sun.
        saint joan. each line
          another chain of repeats
        & visions.

i never meant to spell this out, to
   spill it. i tried being difficult
      & not i
   backtrack, apologise.

    thats what needs to be done, she says.
    where were you when i started speaking?

rob mclennan

bagne: postscript

in an episode of the *X-Files* a few years back, fox mulder ruminates on his only real fear of the then-encroaching millennium: the return of drawstring pants. for thousands of years, history has repeated, & then again. the chinese didn't record historical events for thousands of years, simply on the basis of seeing the cycle, that everything would return back to that same familiar point. for just as long, cultural bursts have attuned their own fears against (apparently) arbitrary marks & tides of doom, so well documented by such texts as Mark Kingwell's brilliant *Dreams of Millennium*. the end is nigh.

bagne, or Criteria for Heaven, was written as a response to that swell. a reaction, perhaps. of the arbitrariness of the triple zero score & the movement that occurred despite reason, & the subsequent hangover that would happen the following morn. as kurt vonnegut once wrote of the year 2000, come & gone & nothing happened, "God is not heavily into numerology."

the resulting text, built in ninety-three interconnected poems, move through history, religion, mass culture, & the immediate "I/eye"; through shifting voices & the unknown "she", ever permanent. taking each title from the last line of another author's poem (& so credited, for/from, by author, not work — let the future essay writers figure those things out), & rolling ahead, each new thread pulling against the rest. this is very much a millennium book, of the constructions that free & restrain us, as the title tells (bagne = prison, labour camp), not only through the day-to-day but throughout. as the two-faced god Janus, looking back, & ahead at once. (you have to learn the rules before you can break them.) published here, in the grey year between centuries makes it so much more appropriate, as society deemed the 20th century over on december 31st, 1999 (making it the shortest century on record), as the 21st doesn't begin until january 1st, 2001. this is the year that doesn't count, the arbitrary post-as-script separating property. belonging to neither, & both. here, we can get away with anything we want.

rob mclennan
ottawa, ontario
march 2000

about the author

rob mclennan is an Ottawa-based poet, visual artist, book reviewer & editor/publisher of *STANZAS* magazine & above/ground press, coordinator of The Factory reading series, the small press action network-Ottawa (SPAN-O) & the ottawa small press book fair. the author of over two dozen poetry chapbooks, & four full collections, the last of which, *The Richard Brautigan Ahhhhhhhhhhh*, was shortlisted for the Archibald Lampman Award, rob is also the editor of *Written in the Skin*, which Montreal's *HOUR* weekly called "one of the 10 best books of 1998" & the anthology *Shadowy Technicians: New Ottawa Poets*, the first title in the cauldron books series he edits with Broken Jaw Press. in 1999, he won the CAA/Air Canada Award for most promising writer in Canada under the age of 30. in March 2000, his first solo show of paintings, *27 people i never want to see again*, appeared at Gamma Ray Productions in Ottawa, just a few short blocks away from his house. he is currently completing a novel & a long poem called "hazelnut". rob can be reached via e-mail at az421@freenet.carleton.ca

rob mclennan

about the cover artist

Over the frenzied course of his career, Tom Fowler's work has appeared on CD and book covers as well as in CD-ROMs and dozens of role-playing games. Shifting his focus to comics, Tom's work has appeared in Oni Press' *The Honor Rollers* (with writer Paul Dini), and a "Jar Jar Binks" story for Dark Horse Comics' *Star Wars Tales* (with Ryder Windham).

He is currently hard at work on the the third issue of the wildly popular *Blair Witch Chronicles* (with Jen Van Meter), again for Oni, and the first of four fully-painted bandes dessinées for Swiss publisher Éditions Paquet, which will eventually see print in English.

Tom Fowler lives and works in Ottawa with his girlfriend, a massive collection of stuff, and a tenuous hold on reality.

A Selection of Our Titles in Print

Title	ISBN	Price
A Lad from Brantford (David Adams Richards) essays	0-921411-25-1	11.95
All the Other Phil Thompsons Are Dead (Phil Thompson) poetry	1-896647-05-7	12.95
A View from the Bucket: A Grand Lake and McNabs Island Memoir (Jean Redekopp) memoir, history	0-921411-52-9	14.95
Best in Life: A Guide to Managing Your Relationships ... (Ted Mouradian) self-development, business	0-921411-55-3	18.69
CHSR Poetry Slam (Andrew Titus, ed.) poetry	1-896647-06-5	10.95
Combustible Light (Matt Santateresa) poetry	0-921411-97-9	12.95
Cover Makes a Set (Joe Blades) poetry	0-919957-60-9	8.95
Crossroads Cant (Mary Elizabeth Grace, Mark Seabrook, Shafiq, Ann Shin. Joe Blades, ed.) poetry	0-921411-48-0	13.95
Dark Seasons (Georg Trakl; Robin Skelton, trans.) poetry	0-921411-22-7	10.95
Dividing the Fire (Robert B. Richards) poetry	1-896647-15-4	4.95
Elemental Mind (K.V. Skene) poetry	1-896647-16-2	10.95
for a cappuccino on Bloor (kath macLean) poetry	0-921411-74-X	13.95
Gift of Screws (Robin Hannah) poetry	0-921411-56-1	12.95
Heaven of Small Moments (Allan Cooper) poetry	0-921411-79-0	12.95
Herbarium of Souls (Vladimir Tasic) short fiction	0-921411-72-3	14.95
I Hope It Don't Rain Tonight (Phillip Igloliorti) poetry	0-921411-57-X	11.95
Like Minds (Shannon Friesen) short fiction	0-921411-81-2	14.95
Manitoba highway map (rob mclennan) poetry	0-921411-89-8	13.95
Memories of Sandy Point, St. George's Bay, Newfoundland (Phyllis Pieroway) memoir, history	0-921411-33-2	14.95
New Power (Christine Lowther) poetry	0-921411-94-4	11.95
Notes on drowning (rob mclennan) poetry	0-921411-75-8	13.95
Open 24 Hours (Anne Burke, D.C. Reid, Brenda Niskala Joe Blades, rob mclennan) poetry	0-921411-64-2	13.95
Railway Station (karl wendt) poetry	0-921411-82-0	11.95
Reader be Thou Also Ready (Robert James) novel	1-896647-26-X	18.69
Rum River (Raymond Fraser) short fiction	0-921411-61-8	16.95
Seeing the World with One Eye (Edward Gates) poetry	0-921411-69-3	12.95
Shadowy:Technicians: New Ottawa Poets (rob mclennan, ed.)	0-921411-71-5	16.95
Song of the Vulgar Starling (Eric Miller) poetry	0-921411-93-6	14.95
Speaking Through Jagged Rock (Connie Fife) poetry	0-921411-99-5	12.95
Tales for an Urban Sky (Alice Major) poetry	1-896647-11-1	13.95
The Longest Winter (Julie Doiron, Ian Roy) photos & fiction	0-921411-95-2	18.69
Túnel de proa verde / Tunnel of the Green Prow (Nela Rio; Hugh Hazelton, translator) poetry	0-921411-80-4	13.95
Unfolding Fern (Robert B. Richards) poetry	0-921411-98-7	3.00
Wharves and Breakwaters of Yarmouth County, Nova Scotia (Sarah Petite) art/nonfiction	1-896647-13-8	17.95
What Morning Illuminates (Suzanne Hancock) poetry	1-896647-18-9	4.95
What Was Always Hers (Uma Parameswaran) fiction	1-896647-12-X	17.95

www.brokenjaw.com hosts our current catalogue, submissions guidelines, maunscript award competitions, booktrade sales representation and distribution information. Broken Jaw Press eBook editions of some titles are also available. Directly from us, all individual orders must be prepaid. All Canadian orders must add 7% GST/HST (Canada Customs and Revenue Agency Number: 12489 7943 RT0001).

BROKEN JAW PRESS, Box 596 Stn A, Fredericton NB E3B 5A6, Canada